# The Mystery of the Picture
# Where did the Universe come from?
# Did it come from nothing?
## With Mary-Katherine, the Young Apologist

## A Young Apologist Detectives' Mystery
### Proving God Exists Series, Book I

**By**
**Mary-Katherine Mammen**
**&**
**Neil Mammen**

***Illustrated by Manuela Soriani***

**The Mystery of the Picture**
**Where did the Universe come from? Did it come from nothing?**
**With Mary-Katherine, the Young Apologist**
**A Young Apologist Detectives' Mystery**
**Proving God Exists Series, Book I**
**by Mary-Katherine Mammen and Neil Mammen, Illustrated by Manuela Soriani**


***Contact the authors at: Neil_MK@NoBlindFaith.com***



For the authors' Evangelistic Christian doctrinal beliefs please refer to www.NoBlindFaith.com

**Published in the United States and Canada by**
**Rational Free Press**
**PO Box 8321, San Jose, CA 95155-8321**
**www.RationalFreePress.com**

***Other Books by the same author/s:***

*Who is Agent X: Proving Science and Logic Show it's More Rational to Think God Exists.* Rational Free Press, 2009. An easy to read book to discuss with your atheist friends with logical and rational answers. Available at www.NoBlindFaith.com

*40 Days Towards a More Godly Nation.* Rational Free Press 2012. A 40 day series for Churches, find out more at www.40DaysToAGodlyNation.com

Quantity copies of this book can be purchased at large discounts at *www.JesusIsInvolvedinPolitics.com*

The motto of the Young Apologist Detectives' Club is:
**Evangelization, Relationship, Investigation, Theology, Apologetics,**
**No Blind Faith!**

**My name is:**

**My Club number is:**

**My YAC ID/Badge number is:**

**Special thanks to the kids of Calvary Christian Academy, San Jose, CA**
Anais-Rose Purchase, Emma Rieger, Grace Brown, Katie Shilk, Kayla Layton, Maddie Krugman, Miles Clarke, Thomas Coffaro, Tommy Holguin, Tristan Mungia
**& their wonderful teacher Mrs. Joanie Rieger**

**Mary-Katherine and her friend Arianna** were having an after school play date over at MK's house. Both girls were members of the Young Apologist Detectives' Club.

**An Apologist is someone who proves Christianity is true and is not just a blind faith.** Once a week, after school they have a club meeting and usually take assignments to do some detective work to find out the truth about Christianity. Today something very interesting happened at the club so they are talking about it as they draw some pictures.

"Hi girls!" said MK's Dad, as he walked into the room, "Have you been leaving your paintings around the house?"

"Hi Mr. Mammen" said Arianna.

"Dad," said Mary-Katherine, "Arianna told us at the Young Apologist Detectives' Club that her brother came home from college today and announced that he doesn't think there is a God anymore."

"Yes," Arianna eagerly exclaimed, "he said his professors taught him that."

MK's dad replied, "Oh, that's interesting. What did your Dad say Arianna?"

"My dad was very unhappy." Arianna did not look happy either. "He said that my brother needed to read the Bible more."

**"What did the Y.A.D. Club members say at your meeting?"** MK's dad was always interested in what the kids in the club were thinking about.

MK responded, "Well, we agreed that it doesn't make sense to just say, 'Read the Bible.'"

"Why not?"

Arianna looked glum, ""Because if my brother doesn't believe in God, that means he also doesn't believe that the Bible is true anymore. Because it's from the Bible that we learn about God. So I don't think reading it *more* will help him change his mind."

"Good point!" MK's Dad was thoughtful. "Girls, let me ask you this. If God is real, would the Bible be the only place where we can discover that?"

The girls looked at each other for a moment. Then MK jumped in, "No, there would be lots of things."

"Like what?"

"Like everything He made," said MK, "Like when I draw a picture"

Her Dad responded, "Exactly, the art will always reveal clues about the artist, especially if the artist wants it to."

**He paused, "I notice that you kids are drawing some art too?"**

"Yes, Dad do you like it?"

"It's very nice. You both are talented and by practicing you'll develop those talents. In fact I've been finding these other pictures all over the house." Her dad waved the pictures he had been carrying. "These don't look like yours."

MK looked at the pictures in his hand, "You are right, we didn't draw these pictures. Besides those are paintings."

"Mommy said she didn't create them either. So who painted them?" He handed them the pictures.

Arianna looked at the pictures with a puzzled expression, "I wouldn't know."

**"Maybe those pictures made themselves?" suggested MK's Dad.**

"You are being silly, Daddy," Mary-Katherine laughed, "nothing can make itself!"

"Why not?" asked her Dad with a grin.

"Because" said MK, "It would have to be there first to make itself, but that's just crazy, because then it would already be there and it wouldn't have to be made, would it?"

Her Dad laughed, "Exactly, so we can figure out that nothing can make itself." He looked over, "Look, there's another picture by the dining table. Did you gals paint that one?"

The girls ran over to look at the new picture.

"No, Dad, that does not look like one of our pictures." said MK.

Her Dad walked over and picked up the picture.

Blind Faith

**"I wonder who painted this picture!** If this picture can't come from itself, maybe it came from nothing?"

"But, nothing can come from nothing?" replied MK with a wise look.

"Why not?" wondered her friend.

"Maybe it's possible, but we've never seen anything else come from nothing. Right Dad?"

Her Dad nodded, "Yes, that's true! For example, science includes the study of nature, but all science is based on the idea that nothing happens on its own. Everything that has a beginning has a cause. Only things that have existed forever need no cause. If new things and events happened on their own all the time, why waste time studying science? Yet people who believe there is no God have to believe that some things that began to exist had *no* cause."

**MK said, "I don't get that, because it makes no sense.** If we believe that new things can come from nothing then we are believing it with blind faith. The motto of the Young Apologist Detectives' Club is 'No Blind Faith.' And anyway, if things happen by nothing for no reason, why would I want to be a scientist. That would be rather silly wouldn't it? Imagine you were a famous scientist and when people said, why does lighting strike and you said '–oh it just happens out of nothing for no reason'. They'd all think you were being funny or are a very bad scientist."

Arianna laughed, "And imagine if you were a detective investigating a crime and you said 'nobody did that crime, it just happened on it's own.' They'd know you were a very bad detective."

"The more good scientists and detectives the better," nodded MK's Dad. "But wouldn't it also be a bad idea to just say God did it?"

"Yes, but not if you could prove it!" replied Mary-Katherine.

Her Dad smiled.

**He looked at the large Grandfather Clock,** "OK the mystery is to find out who made these paintings, but we have a few minutes before dinner, do you girls want to go outside and look at the skies?"

Theology Apologetics Relationship
Rational Faith

**They trooped outside.** The night was warm and clear with no clouds.

"Wow, look at all the stars and galaxies" said Arianna as they sat down on the cool dry grass.

MK's dad pointed up, "Do you see Orion's Belt? All of those stars are bigger than our earth and most are bigger than our own Sun."

"Wow" said MK.

**"OK girls, where did the very very very first thing that ever was, come from?"** asked MK's Dad.'

Both girls looked puzzled. "Think it through," he encouraged.

There was a long pause.

MK finally said, "It must have always been there."

"Why?"prompted her Dad.

"Well," said MK, "Something can't come from nothing. So if something is there, then something had to always be there. Otherwise the very first thing would never have begun to be there in the first place."

"I don't get it." Arianna had a confused look on her face.

**"Well, if nothing comes from nothing, and nothing can make itself, then where did the very first thing come from?"** MK was using her 'teaching' voice.

"Oh of course, it wouldn't have anything or anywhere to come from so nothing would be there, unless it was always there." said Arianna, her face clearing up.

"Exactly," said MK's Dad, "For anything to be at all, something had to exist forever and ever, that is, it had to have been there forever. It couldn't come from anywhere and nothing could come before it."

"But" Arianna complained, "How can something just be there forever and never come from anywhere? I can't even imagine that."

**"Well" said MK's Dad,** "Philosophically speaking, there are things that can exist forever. It's true that we can't easily conceive of how something cannot have a start and or how something could have just have been there forever. And yes, we have a lot of trouble imagining it. But it is very scientific and it *is* very logical – that means it makes sense."

**They walked up a little hill and stood looking up at the stars.**

Without taking her eyes off the galaxies, Arianna asked, "Mr. Mammen, where did all this ...everything... come from, has all this been around forever?"

MK's dad said, "We call 'everything' the Universe. That includes the World, the Sun, the stars, the planets, the galaxies, and everything in outer space. They are all inside the Universe."

"Including our Earth and you and me?" asked MK.

"Yes, everything."

**There was a pause for a minute.**

Then Mary-Katherine said "Wow! Everything."

They continued to look up at "everything" for a long time.

**Finally Arianna asked softly,** "So where did everything .... the Universe come from? Has everything always been here?"

"Actually no," MK's Dad shook his head thoughtfully, "for centuries scientists claimed the univese was eternally old and the Bible was wrong. But scientific research in the last 80 years indicates that the Universe began to exist at some point in time. Our experiments and observations show the universe is not infinite and is expanding. It's not infinitely old and it's not infinitely big."

Mary-Katherine asked, "What does infinite mean?"

"It means never ending. So the Universe is not never-ending, it's not eternally old and it's not ever-lasting."

**"So if the Universe began and hasn't been around forever, then that means someone had to make the universe,"** said MK.

"Or some-*thing*." said Arianna.

MK replied, "Maybe not something, because Dad, remember you once told me that it could not be some-*thing*, because *things* can't think. So a thing can't decide to do something different like make a Universe when there wasn't one before.

"Good memory Honey." replied her Dad, "A machine with no mind could not have made our universe unless our universe was infinitely old or unless there were infinite other universes. But, the universe is not infinitely old and no one can prove that there are infinite other universes. However, I'll have to explain all that another time[1].

**"So," said MK "People would have to have blind faith to believe that a thing made the universe."**

Her Dad looked at them, "Yes, let's look at the clues we have. 1. The Universe could not have made itself. 2. It's unscientific and silly to think nothing made the Universe and finally 3. Since a thing without a mind could not have made the Universe, what does that mean? Where did it all come from?"

"It means somebody had to make the universe?" concluded Arianna.

---

1 MK's note: YAD Club members, please see Book II in this series.

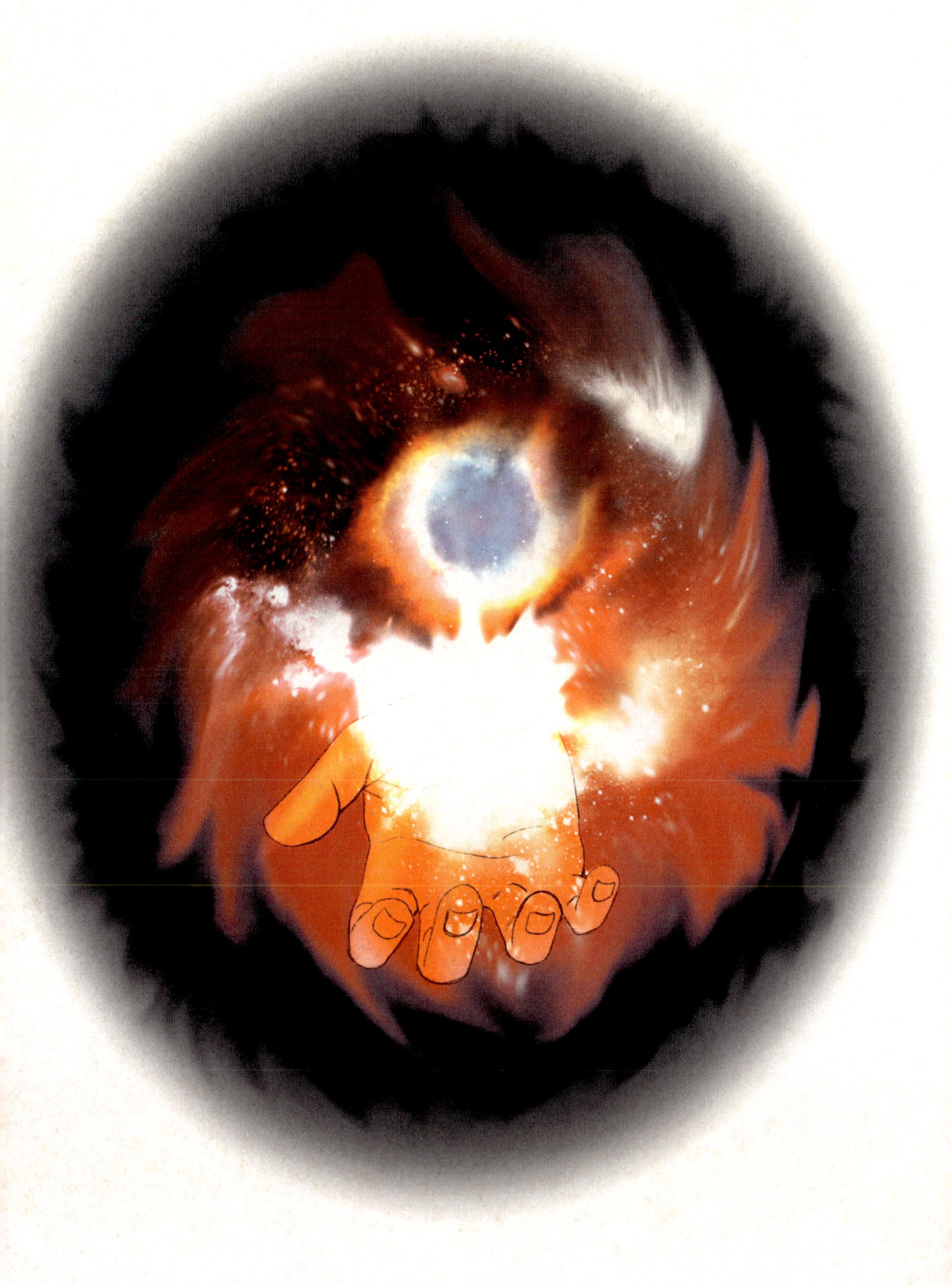

**"Yes, but don't forget that it had to be somebody who has enough power to make a Universe,"** added MK's Dad.

MK noted, "That means only God could have made the  Universe."

Dad said, "Well, we can logically say that only an eternal all-powerful being with a free will and a mind could have made the Universe."

MK said, "Dad isn't that just a fancy way of saying God?"

"Actually...yes. Though there are some more things I will need to explain to you first, to prove that. Remember we don't want to just say: God did it. We'll have to talk about that later. Right now I hear your Mom calling us for dinner. But remember this, there are many ways to prove God exists without using the Bible; one of them is to understand where all of creation came from, the other ways are to look at philosophy, history, logic and reason."

**The girls and MK's Dad walked back into the house.**

Suddenly MK's Dad said, "Look, there's another picture."

The girls ran to it.

MK's Dad said, "So if the picture can't make itself and a picture can't come from nothing ...then..."

Arianna chimed in "...then someone must have made the picture."

MK's Dad smiled, "Why couldn't it have been a computer?"

MK said, "Because a computer is a thing, a machine, and can't think for itself. Even if it came from a computer, a person with a mind must have first programmed the computer. So if the picture was printed by a computer, what thinking person made it print the picture?"

**MK picked up the picture and looked at it carefully,** "But this is a picture that a person painted. And we know that the art reveals the artist. We can tell by this art, that this artist is just learning to paint. Who is the only one around here who is just learning to paint?"

**She paused and looked around.** "Who else, but little Charlotte. And there she *is*, painting another picture."

Little Charlotte squealed and ran into her father's arms giggling.

MK laughed: "We caught you mystery artist. Gotcha!"

"Another Young Apologetics Detectives' Mystery solved!" declared Arianna. "We'll have to explain our detective work to the other Young Apologetics Detectives at the next meeting."

**Later that night as she was going to bed,** after they'd read the Bible and prayed, MK was thoughtful, "Dad, if everything in the universe began to exist, that means it was all made."

"Yes."

"Then" continued MK, "that means everything is art. But God was never made, because he existed for ever, so that makes Him the Original Artist doesn't it?"

"That's very wise thinking" nodded her Dad.

Mary-Katherine snuggled into his arms.

A few moments later, her Dad kissed her head and said softly, "And you are one of His most beautiful works of art."

But Mary-Katherine was already asleep.

***Next book in this Series:***
***What kind of Being made the Universe? The Mystery of the Unknown Sound.***

## Young Apologist Detectives' Club
## Weekly Meeting Discussion Questions

Each week pick a different member
who wants to lead the discussion.

1. What is the motto of the Young Apologist Detective's Club?
2. Why is it hard to use the Bible to prove God exists to someone who does not believe in God?
3. Where else besides the Bible can we find out about God?
4. Where did the first thing or being that ever was, come from?
5. For anything to exist, something must what?
6. Could a robot make itself? Why not?
7. Could a computer make itself? Why not?
8. Why can't something make itself?
9. Can something come from nothing?
10. If part of science is the study of why things happen, do you think a scientist who just says something came from nothing is a good scientist?
11. Should we automatically say that "God did it?" when we can't explain something? When can we say "God did it?"
12. What is the Universe?
13. Has the Universe been around forever?
14. If the Universe has not been around forever what can we know about what made it?
15. What does Infinite mean?
16. How does the painting relate to God in this story?
17. How does the painting relate to the Universe and "Everything" in this story?
18. Can a painting paint itself?
19. Have you ever seen anything in nature that seems like a painting or art?
20. What if someone says everything came naturally? What would you ask them?
21. Do you know anybody who doesn't believe in God?
22. Why do you think they don't believe in God?

**Go on line to www.NoBlindFaith.com to find the answers.**

## Some conclusions

1. Nothing can come from nothing.

2. If anything exists, some *thing* or some *being* must have existed forever.

3. This thing that existed forever must be responsible for all things that begin to exist.

4. Nothing can make itself, because to make itself it would already have to exist, in which case why would it need to make itself.

5. The universe has not been around forever.

6. If anyone says things came naturally, you should ask:
"Where did that nature come from?" or "Where did that ability of nature come from?"

7. If someone says "The Universe came from Quantum Fluctuations (or uses some complicated concepts)." You say, "But that isn't nothing." If they say, "Well, nothing isn't actually nothing." You should say "That's not true: nothing is nothing. If it isn't nothing then it's something. What exactly is that something? Let's find out what it is? (In the next book we'll explain why thingss like Quantum Fluctuations won't work.")

8. Science is the study of nature and why things happen.
If someone says something came about for no reason then they are not being scientific.

9. Someone may ask: "But if everything needs a cause, and nothing happens on it's own, then where did God come from?" The answer is that, only things that ***begin*** to exist need a cause. Anything that has existed forever needs no cause. Remember God didn't ***happen***. He's always existed. And as we figured out something had to exist forever for ***anything*** to exist at all. With more investigation we can deduce who or what that "something" is. Read the rest of the mysteries in this series to find out.

## End Notes and References

Dear Parent, statistics indicate that maybe 75% or more of all Christian kids abandon their faith in college. This ought to be a serious concern for all Christian parents, sadly it often isn't. Many kids leave High School with an emotional faith in Christ, but not an intellectual or scientific one.

When these kids get to college those emotions are replaced by new emotions and many kids are talked out of their faith by their new heroes; atheistic and secular professors. After all, they've been sent to college by their parents to be taught by these very professors.

**The Young Apologist Detectives' Mystery Series** is intended to introduce Apologetics to kids. Apologetics is the proof of the Evidence for the truth of Christianity using science, logic, facts, history and philosophy.

This book is the first in the "Proving God exists without using the Bible" series for kids aged 6 and above.

May we suggest you encourage your kids to start a Young Apologist Detectives' Club (for around ages 6-12) in their Church and School or even just amongst their friends. Then use these materials and others to immunize them against the attacks they will face in College. The clubs are intended to be run by the kids themselves with adult supervision only as needed and on occasion. We want the kids to take responsibility for their inquiries and detective work themselves, so they get used to doing the research on their own before accepting someone else's conclusions. Parents are encouraged to let kids ask the toughest questions about Christianity and then should work with the kids to ***lead*** them to the answers.

## Starting a Young Apologist Detectives' Club

Go to www.NoBlindFaith.com to order the materials or get on our mailing list to know when the materials will be available.

When your children start their own Young Apologist Detectives' Club they will get a Young Apologist Detectives' Club Badge, a Young Apologist Detectives' Club Manual and a Young Apologist Detectives' Club ID. The Young Apologists Detective Badge and Manual and ID is $15. Each badge comes with the Detective's unique serial number. In addition they will get Special Apologetics Projects to do and a number of online video messages for kids targeted at their age group. Membership and access to the videos is only $30 (one time fee and can be shared within a club with the Club access number).

**More books and resources can be found at www.NoBlindFaith.com**

This book has one rather complex point which kids may have difficulty understanding. That is the concept introduced by the footnote on page 16. The idea that only a being with a freewill could create a universe that wasn't either eternally old, or just one of infinite other universes. This is based on the idea discussed later i.e. the printer that prints a picture on their own. This concept is flushed out in the next book in the series.

To find out more as an adult and to help answer your kid's questions please consider getting the detailed book written for adults: *Who is Agent X? Proving science and logic show it's more reasonable to think God exists*, 2009, Rational Free Press, available on our website.

*This book was co-written by Mary-Katherine Mammen who was 7 at the time. Mary-Katherine came up with many of the ideas, the storyline and parts of the dialog as well as determined what the pictures should be.*

## My Notes

**signed:**

# My Deductions

**signed:**

Made in the USA
Middletown, DE
12 October 2021

50190887R00015